Stuff the Quiche

Stuff the Quiche

Peter Coupe

INDEX

Published by Arcturus Publishing Limited
For Index,
Unit 1
Garrard Way
Kettering
NN16 8TD

This edition published 1996

Printed and bound in Great Britain

ISBN 1 900032 46 5

If you've always had a suspicion that the "New Man" is a bit like a UFO – often talked about but never actually seen – then this collection of cartoons is for you!

'Stuff the Quiche' covers every aspect of men's worst behaviour, and whether you buy this book for yourself or have it thrust upon you by the woman in your life, you are almost certain to find yourself in it somewhere.

In 'Stuff the Quiche' you will see men in their true colours; dealing with important issues like sex and marriage, and trying to work out how to get one without the other.

Only the names have been changed – *to protect the guilty!*

FUNNY THING...
...MY HEADACHE'S GONE!

BUT YOU CAN'T HAVE BEEN WITH CAROL LAST NIGHT, BECAUSE I... ER... ERM..

I'M NEVER GOING TO HAVE THE BODY OF A GREEK GOD – NO MATTER HOW MANY BURNT OFFERINGS YOU GIVE ME!!

HOW CAN IT BE BIGAMY – I NEVER MARRIED EITHER OF YOU MORE THAN ONCE...

HIS WIFE RAN OFF WITH HIS BEST FRIEND – BUT *SHE* CAME BACK . . .

WHEN YOU'RE UNDRESSED JUST PUT YOUR CLOTHES ON THE CHAIR WITH MINE, MISS. BROWN!

I JOINED ALCOHOLICS ANONYMOUS – NOW I CAN DRINK USING ANOTHER NAME...

WELL IT MAY WELL BE HOW YOU DO IT FOR YOUR WIFE, MR. SMITH, BUT IT ISN'T HOW WE MAKE A STIFF DRINK HERE...

I'VE BEEN CALCULATING...
... THIS TROLLEY COSTS
£1,653 A MILE TO RUN!

THE 'LITTLE BOY LOST' ACT
CERTAINLY WORKS FOR JIM...

WELL - IF YOU DIDN'T ASK ME QUESTIONS
I WOULDN'T HAVE TO TELL LIES...

YOU'VE GOT YOUR HANDBAG UNDER YOUR SEAT AGAIN HAVEN'T YOU!?

HE HASN'T SPOKEN TO HER FOR TWO YEARS-
HE'S FAR TOO POLITE TO INTERRUPT !

CALL IT THE MALE MENOPAUSE IF YOU LIKE - BUT EITHER THE DRESSING GOWN GOES, OR I GO!

GEOFF'S VERY SPORTY - HE DOESN'T MIND WHAT POSITION WE MAKE LOVE IN, AS LONG AS HE CAN STILL SEE THE FOOTBALL ON T.V...

I MARRIED HIM FOR HIS 'COME TO BED' EYES - NOW THEY GO WITHOUT ME...

–ARE YOU THE FIRST WOMAN I EVER MADE LOVE TO?
IT'S POSSIBLE – YOUR FACE IS CERTAINLY FAMILIAR!

MY WIFE IS GREAT IN BED ... ASK ANYONE!

AN ORGASM? I OVERHEARD YOUR SISTER SAYING SHE'D HAD ONE...
CAN'T YOU JUST BORROW HERS...

OF COURSE I DON'T SAY THAT TO ALL THE GIRLS...

...ONLY THE ONES WHO LET ME SLEEP WITH THEM!

THERE WAS NO REASON TO REPORT IT EARLIER –
THERE WAS PLENTY OF FOOD IN THE FREEZER...

INLAND REVENUE STAFF
CHRISTMAS FANCY DRESS PARTY

I LOVE YOU TERRIBLY, EDWINA, BUT I'M SURE I'LL GET BETTER IF YOU'LL ALLOW ME TO PRACTISE A LITTLE MORE OFTEN...

JACK WAS LISTENING TO THE NEWLYWED COUPLE NEXT DOOR LAST NIGHT—AND HE'S DECIDED THEY COULD DO WITH A FEW TIPS …

DON'T BE STUPID! SNAILS DON'T GET DIVORCED—THEY JUST CHANGE SEX!

WOW! I DIDN'T REALISE IDENTICAL TWINS DID EVERYTHING TOGETHER!!

-CAN WE DO HALF A DOZEN WELL-STACKED LEGGY BIMBOs FOR THE RUGBY CLUB DINNER-DANCE NEXT SATURDAY!
COMPULOVE DATING AGENCY.

WHAT FLAVOUR CONDOMS DO YOU WANT THIS WEEKEND, DARLING?!
SHAMPOO

-THIS NEW TELEVISION SEX CHANNEL IS RUBBISH -EVERY TIME THEY GET TO AN INTERESTING BIT THEY TURN THE LIGHT OFF!

HIS WIFE THREATENED TO LEAVE HIM IF HE CARRIED ON DRINKING—HE'S BEEN HERE EVERSINCE...

–I'M GETTING MARRIED AT THE WEEKEND – IS THAT LONG ENOUGH TO PROVIDE ME WITH A CHEQUERED PAST ?!

YOU WANT TO DO IT THE OTHER WAY ROUND? WELL – I'M NOT GETTING UP TO MOVE THE BED AT THIS TIME OF NIGHT!

..OF COURSE I'M NOT COMPARING YOU WITH MY MOTHER – I'D GET MY IRONING DONE IF I WAS!

MATERNITY
RECEPTION
WELL-
APART FROM
ONE BIT
AT LEAST!
MARVO
THE
RUBBER
MAN

I EVEN HATED QUICHE WHEN IT WAS PLAIN EGG AND BACON FLAN!

DRUNK ??
HEAVENS NO! THAT'S
MR. WRIGLY FROM
ACCOUNTS –
HE'S A PERVERT!

IO
IOU

PHHWORR!

I THINK DIARIES ARE SO OLD-FASHIONED...

IT'S YOUR WIFE - SHE SUSPECTS YOU'RE HAVING AN AFFAIR WITH SOMEONE, AND SHE WANT'S ME TO KEEP AN EYE ON YOU...

EAT AT JOES
MAYBE THERE IS TOO MUCH SEX IN ADVERTISING THESE DAYS...

HOW-EXACTLY-IS ME ASKING FOR HELP WITH WASHING UP SEXUAL HARASSMENT?

IT'S QUITE FUNNY REALLY... HOW YOU GET IT WRONG ON THE VERY LAST SENTENCE EVERY TIME...
SEX-SEX-SEX-SEX
TAKE 53

–OF COURSE YOU CAN IF YOU WANT TO…
…BUT I THOUGHT YOU HATED JOGGING!

ROMANCE
SEX
THE REAL DIFFERENCE BETWEEN MEN AND WOMEN?!

MY MARRIAGE ENDED IN SICKNESS AND DEATH . . .

. . . MY WIFE GOT SICK TO DEATH OF ME!

HOW MANY TIMES HAVE I TOLD YOU NOT TO SNEAK UP BEHIND ME LIKE THAT!

AFTER SHAVE
... SOMETHING THAT SMELLS SEXY AFTER 7 PINTS OF LAGER AND A VINDALOO...

POOR CHAP!
SINCE HIS WIFE LEFT HE SPENDS ALL HIS TIME IN THAT GARDEN SHED...
...MUST GET TERRIBLY LONELY!

YES – THESE DATING AGENCY DETAILS CAN BE A LITTLE MISLEADING – I'D SAY MORE ROBERT REDFORD THAN PAUL NEWMAN...

I WISH I'D NEVER ENROLLED YOU IN THAT DAMN RELAXATION CLASS!

HE HAD AN IMPORTANT DARTS MATCH...
...AND CAN WE RESET THE VIDEO TO RECORD THE BIG MATCH WHEN WE'RE FINISHED!
MARRIAGE GUIDANCE

-AND NOW - IN THE LINGERIE SECTION OF YOUR T.V. SHOPPING CHANNEL...

HIS LAST GIRLFRIEND WAS IN CONSUMER PROTECTION ~
SHE PROSECUTED HIM UNDER THE WEIGHTS AND MEASURES ACT !

BOY!! THAT WAS ONE HELL OF A TARTS AND VICARS PARTY LAST NIGHT!

OF COURSE I'VE TAKEN PRECAUTIONS – MY WIFE THINKS I'M PLAYING SNOOKER AND I'VE GIVEN YOU A FALSE NAME !

YOU SAID TAKE THE BABY TO THE PARK - YOU DIDN'T SAY ANYTHING ABOUT BRINGING IT BACK AGAIN.

BUT I ONLY HAD AN AFFAIR SO YOU WOULDN'T FEEL I WAS TAKING YOU FOR GRANTED!

THE DOCTOR'S PUT HIM ON A STRENUOUS NEW FITNESS REGIME...

... HE'S CONFISCATED THE REMOTE!

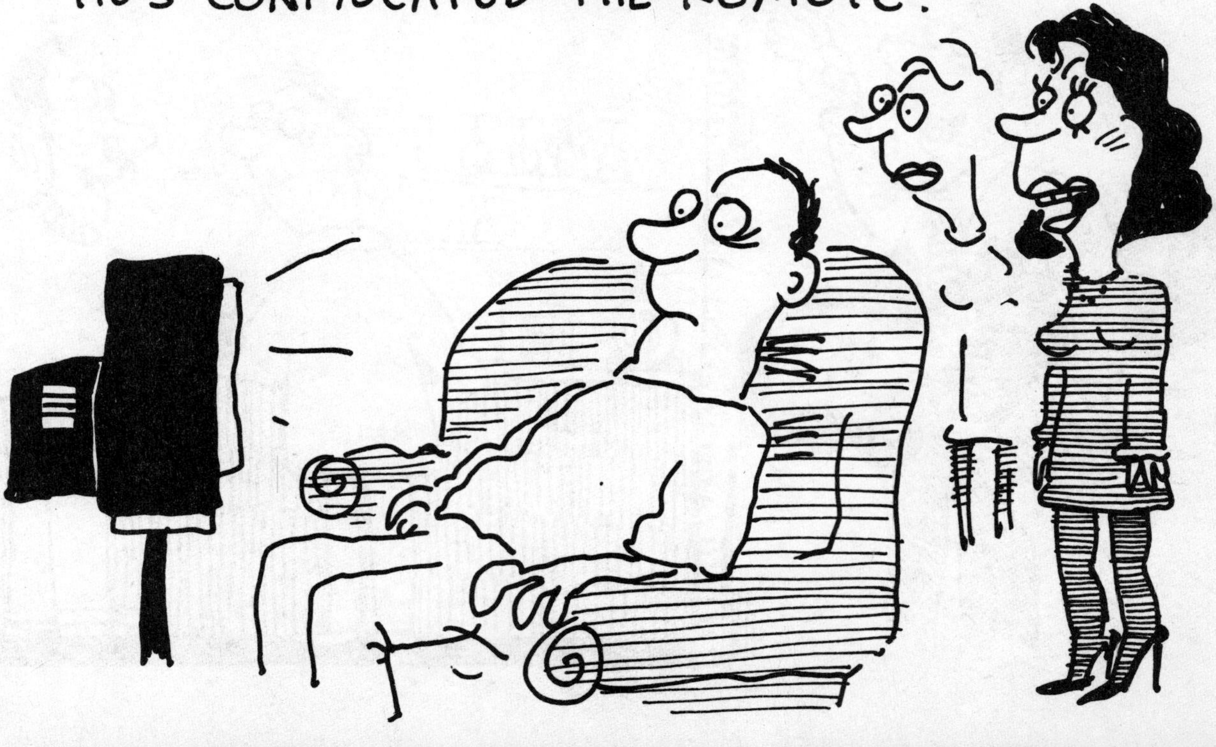

JACK'S BRINGING HIS NEW GIRLFRIEND IN TONIGHT – HE SAYS SHE'S A **MODEL**!

–I'D LOVE TO COME – BUT MY HUSBAND HAS VERY FIXED IDEAS ABOUT A WOMAN'S PLACE...

- CHECK OUT THOSE SPECIAL QUICK RELEASE VELCRO PATCHES!
FLASHAMAC

– OF COURSE WE'RE PRACTISING SAFE SEX – BUT IT'S GOING TO BE AGES BEFORE WE GET IT PERFECT!

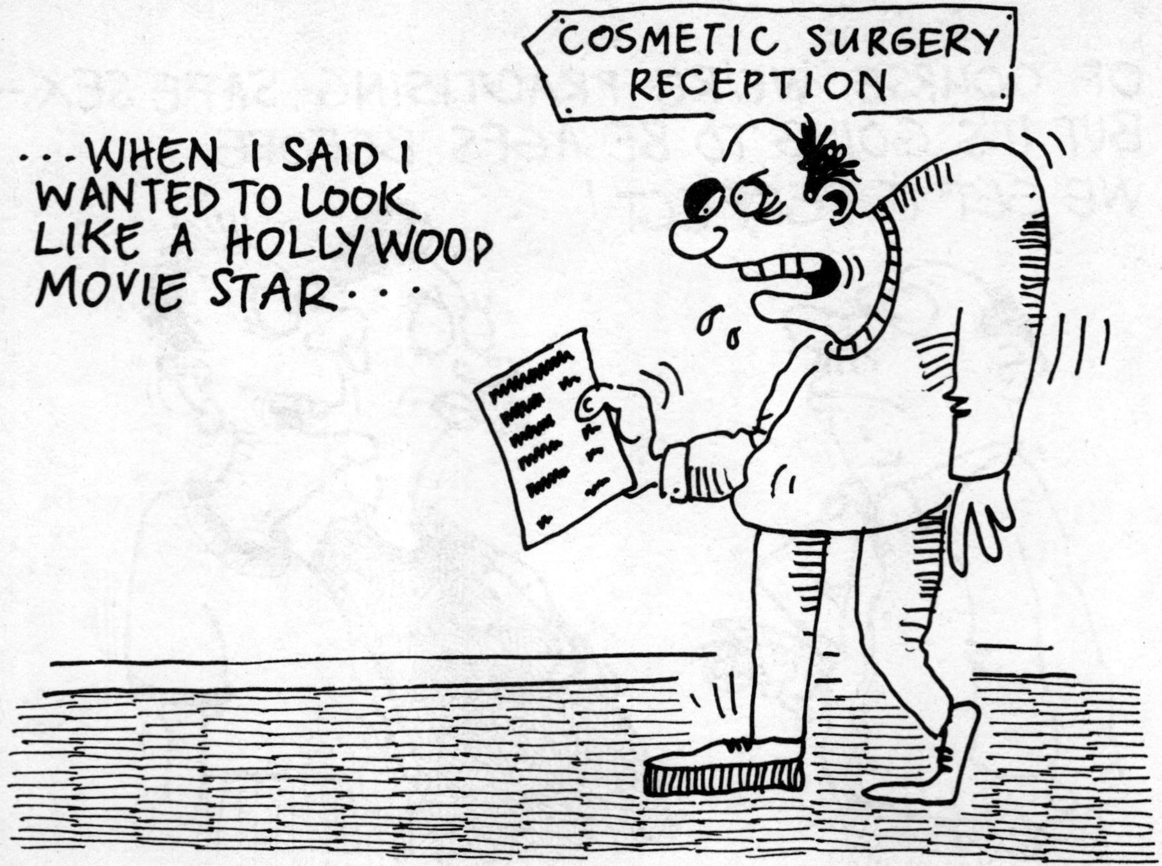
COSMETIC SURGERY
RECEPTION
...WHEN I SAID I
WANTED TO LOOK
LIKE A HOLLYWOOD
MOVIE STAR...

NOW, SON, YOUR MOTHER THINKS YOU'RE OLD ENOUGH FOR ME TO TALK TO YOU ABOUT SEX –

– AND CAN YOU GIVE ME SOME TIPS ?!

I HAD AN EXTRA INCH ADDED FOR EVERY MILLION I WON ON THE LOTTERY!

I TOLD HER 'MUSIC IS THE FOOD OF LOVE'-
SO SHE SET FIRE TO THE STEREO...

- GO AND REMIND MR SCRIMSHAW AND MISS. PUGH THAT THE NEW VIDEO SECURITY SYSTEM IS UP AND RUNNING...

MY WIFE SAYS YOU'RE A STEREOTYPE—
BUT THEN SHE'S NEVER HAD AN EYE FOR MUSIC!

PERSONNEL? CAN YOU PUT OUT AN ADVERT. FOR A NEW SECRETARY FOR ME...
.... MISS BLENKINSOP WILL BE LEAVING TO HAVE A BABY IN THE NOT TOO DISTANT FUTURE...

TO BE HONEST – I DID HAVE MY DOUBTS ABOUT COMPUTER DATING INITIALLY...

DUE TO A NASTY REBOUND IN PRACTISE, I UNDERSTAND.

WE'RE GOING TO BERMUDA THIS SUMMER...
...ALBERT WANTS TO STUDY THE TRIANGLES...

YOU TOLD MY WIFE ABOUT OUR AFFAIR DIDN'T YOU?

I DIDN'T THINK YOU WOULD ENJOY MOTORCYCLING -
WHAT WITH ALL THE NOISE
AND VIBRATION!

I LIKE MY WOMEN TO LIE BACK AND THINK OF ENGLAND-
WHICH IS WHY I NEVER SCORE EITHER...

—NO! I'M NOT FAKING IT. I THOUGHT YOU WERE—
THAT'S WHY I STOPPED TAKING MY PILL!

GOD! I WISH I HAD MY OWN TRANSPORT!

SHE WAS JUST
A GOOD FRIEND...
LOVERS
LEAP

WA-HEY!
NO-WAY!!

YOU LOOK LIKE A WELL EDUCATED YOUNG WOMAN – HOW DO YOU FANCY COMING UP TO MY ROOM TO HELP ME WRITE MY WILL?

BUT YOU CAN'T LEAVE ME – I NEED THOSE SUITCASES FOR MY FISHING TRIP NEXT WEEK...

GAY BAR
OPEN
LET'S HAVE A COUPLE OF PINTS IN THERE - I COULD DO WITH CHEERING UP!

– AND TO THINK – IF I HADN'T BROUGHT MY TOOLKIT WE WOULD NEVER HAVE MET!

MY WIFE HAS THIS CRAZY IDEA THAT I CAN'T BE TRUSTED ... BUT WHY DON'T I TELL YOU ABOUT IT OVER A ROMANTIC CANDLE-LIT DINNER FOR TWO ...

LET'S JUST TAKE TURNS FOR NOW - AND ARGUE ABOUT WHO SLEEPS ON WHICH SIDE OF THE BED WHEN WE GET HOME...

WE'VE HAD TEN VERY, VERY HAPPY YEARS OF MARRIAGE... WHICH ISN'T BAD OUT OF TWENTY SIX...

SEVENTH HEAVEN ISN'T SO GREAT WHEN THE LIFT ISN'T WORKING!..
7

-BUT AT LEAST IT KEEPS HIM OFF THE STREETS...

IT WAS VERY KIND OF YOU TO OFFER ME A BED FOR THE NIGHT –
– YOU MUST LET ME KNOW HOW I CAN REPAY YOU...

- AND IF YOU VOTE
FOR ME I PROMISE TO
CAUSE A SEXUAL SCANDAL
THAT WILL PUT THIS
TOWN ON THE MAP!!

HE'S DOING THE KNOWLEDGE...

WELL, I THOUGHT YOU AND I COULD SORT IT OUT – THEN I COULD TELL HER WHAT SHE HAS TO DO WHEN I GET HOME!

IT HASN'T ALWAYS BEEN LIKE THIS...
...BACK IN THE 60'S I WAS A SEXUAL DYNAMO...

MY HUSBAND WANTS A VIDEO CAMERA TO MAKE SEXY FILMS - AND WE'LL PROBABLY NEED ONE OR TWO EXTRAS...

WE WERE GOING TO LIVE TOGETHER - BUT DECIDED MARRIAGE WOULD BE EASIER TO GET OUT OF IF THINGS DIDN'T WORK OUT...

HE'S BEEN LIKE THIS SINCE I SAID I'D BEND OVER BACKWARDS TO PLEASE HIM IF I COULD GO TO YOGA CLASSES...

DIAMONDS ARE FOREVER – SO I **ASSUME** COLOURED GLASS IS ALRIGHT FOR A ONE-NIGHT STAND ?!

–I'M ALREADY A REGULAR ATTENDER AT A MALE ENCOUNTER GROUP – WE CALL IT THE **RED LION!**

NO! I DIDN'T NOTICE THE CHAMBERMAID'S SEXY BLUE EYES...

– OH, YES, I AGREE. LOVELY LEGS. BUT LOOK AT THE WAY THE DRAWERS ARE HANGING DOWN!

"REFUND AND REPLACE"... YOU NEED THE BIG SUPERMARKET DOWN THE HIGH STREET...
SPERM BANK
TENK

I THOUGHT LONG AND HARD ABOUT THE ENVIRONMENTAL IMPLICATIONS OF BUYING A CAR THAT ONLY DOES 12 MILES TO THE GALLON – THEN I THOUGHT... <u>BUGGER IT</u>!

BATTERY
POWERED
SCREWDRIVERS

- OF COURSE I DON'T DRINK AND DRIVE -
I DON'T NEED TO - I'M MARRIED...

IT'S JUST NOT MY IDEA OF A TOPLESS BAR, THAT'S ALL...

–SHALL WE GO TO BED AND MAKE LOVE – OR WATCH NEIGHBOURS ??

-DAD - THIS IS TRIXIE - SHE'S THE SORT OF GIRL YOU WARNED ME ABOUT...

YES, I KNOW THE BABY'S CRYING –
THAT'S WHAT I WOKE YOU UP TO TELL YOU!

MY WIFE GOT CUSTODY OF THE
CREDIT CARDS!

BATTER ME A LETTUCE – I'M GOING THROUGH A HEALTH-FOOD FAD!

OF COURSE THERE WAS A VACUUM IN MY LIFE WHEN MY WIFE LEFT ME – BUT SHE TOOK THAT A COUPLE OF WEEKS LATER, ALONG WITH THE T.V. AND VIDEO . . .

–AND JUST A PINCH OF TOKEN MAN–

EDEN COSMETIC SURGERY
FIG LEAF
ENLARGEMENT

OH YES! I STILL LOOK AT PRETTY YOUNG GIRLS – TROUBLE IS I CAN'T REMEMBER WHY?!

PLUS ... REMARRIAGE TO THE PARTNER OF YOUR CHOICE – FREE OF CHARGE – WITH OUR NEW ... "TWO FOR THE PRICE OF ONE CARD!

HOW ABOUT COMING ROUND TO MY PLACE FOR A MEAL ··· BREAKFAST PERHAPS ?!...

DO YOU HAVE ANY ANNIVERSARY CARDS THAT AREN'T QUITE SO ENTHUSIASTIC?

I'VE REALLY COME TO HATE THE SUMMER SINCE MY WIFE LEFT...
...YOU HAVE TO IRON THE BACKS OF YOUR SHIRTS AS WELL AS THE FRONTS!

I JUST CAN'T GET ANY SLEEP WITH THE NOISE FROM ALL THE PARTIES GOING ON DOWN THERE!

Dear Jane -
Thank you for
last night - it
was wonderful.
I will be back to
read your meter
again in June.
Love,
Jim x

Your dinner's in the dog

Your dinner's in the dog

Peter Coupe

INDEX

Published by Arcturus Publishing Limited
For Index,
Unit 1
Garrard Way
Kettering
NN16 8TD

This edition published 1996

Printed and bound in Great Britain

ISBN 1 900032 51 1

If you have a “New Man” in your life, but are still having to do all the ironing, shopping and toilet cleaning, this book is for you.

Woman are people after all; and can be as crafty, sly and downright dishonest as men – when it suits them.

This book is definately not a guide to the perfect relationship; but rest assured that it doesn’t contain any recipes or fashion tips either.

In this witty and acerbic collection of cartoons we can see how women finish up on top far more often than the men in their lives would have us believe.

I'VE JUST GOT TO ORGANISE
MR. BLENKINSOP'S WHIP ROUND...

IT'S A WITHDRAWAL SYMPTOM!

-OF COURSE SIZE ISN'T EVERYTHING GERALD - BUT IT DOES HAVE ADVANTAGES IN CERTAIN SITUATIONS...

NO, DARLING, I WON'T FORGET OUR ANNIVERSARY NEXT YEAR...

IS THAT A GUN
IN YOUR POCKET-
OR ARE YOU ONE
OF THOSE MEN WHO
TUCKS HIS SHIRT
INTO HIS
UNDERPANTS?

JUST MAKING THE GARDENER A CUP OF TEA...
... HE'S BEEN HARD AT IT ALL MORNING IN THE FLOWER BED!

PARFUMS
JUST A SMALL BOTTLE – ENOUGH TO SHIFT THE BALANCE OF POWER DURING WIMBLEDON FORTNIGHT!

SOMEONE TOLD ME YOU WERE UP TO YOUR OLD TRICKS AGAIN...

– WHY IS MY WIFE DOWN THERE WITH MR. PHELPS THE MILKMAN?

YOU MAY WELL HAVE A PHOTOGRAPHIC MEMORY - BUT AS FAR AS OUR ANNIVERSARY IS CONCERNED YOU NEED TO HAVE IT DEVELOPED!

WELL, MR. SMITH, I'VE HEARD YOUR WIFE'S SIDE OF THE STORY — AND IT SOUNDS TO ME THAT YOU'VE SOME EXPLAINING TO DO...
MARRIAGE GUIDANCE

BUT OF COURSE MY HUSBAND KNOWS WHERE I AM – I TOLD HIM I WAS GOING OUT TO GET A DISHWASHER!

NO, DARLING, THAT'S NOT THE 'G' SPOT – THAT'S THE HOT WATER BOTTLE!

WELL - CAN I TAKE THE BLINDFOLD OFF NOW AND SEE MY SURPRISE...!?
VASECTOMY CLINIC

...YOU JUST HAVEN'T GOT A CLUE ABOUT EQUALITY HAVE YOU DEREK...

FOR HEAVEN'S SAKE TRY TO BE MORE POSITIVE – THINK HOW MUCH WORSE IT WOULD BE IF YOU HAD TO SLEEP WITH A MALE BOSS TO GET PROMOTION!

YOUR MISTRESS
IS IN THE
HOSPITAL-
YOUR CLOTHES
ARE IN THE
DUSTBIN - YOUR
DINNER'S IN
THE DOG!

OF COURSE I HAVE ORGASMS – BUT YOU TOLD ME NEVER TO CALL YOU AT WORK...

I HAD A LOVELY TIME – BUT GERALD WAS KIDNAPPED BY TERRORISTS ON THE FIRST DAY...

I JUST WANT YOU TO KNOW THAT IF YOU WANT TO SEXUALLY HARASS SOMEONE IN THE WORKPLACE –
I'M HERE FOR YOU!

I DIDN'T SEE HIS
WIFE COME IN...
...DID YOU?

I THINK OUR WORKING RELATIONSHIP
IS QUITE CLOSE ENOUGH
MR. WILKINS!

WELL - I'LL CERTAINLY NEVER DOUBT THE POWER OF WITCHCRAFT AGAIN...

I KNOW HE'S NOT MUCH TO LOOK AT – BUT HE HAS NO INTEREST IN SEX, HELPS WITH THE HOUSEWORK AND CAN ACTUALLY ASSEMBLE A 'FLAT PACKED' WARDROBE KIT!

—CLEANS FLOORS THE EASY WAY!
(ALTHOUGH FOR THE COMMERCIAL WE JUST PUT DOWN NEW LINO OF COURSE ...)
ZAP
CLEANS FLOORS!

MUM, DAD, I'D LIKE TO INTRODUCE THE MAN I'M GOING TO MARRY – BUT AS I HAVEN'T MET HIM YET I'VE BROUGHT ONE OF THE BOYS I'M CURRENTLY HAVING SEX WITH...

-AND I'LL NEED ANOTHER 60 TO SEND TO ALL THE BOYFRIENDS I HAD BEFORE I MARRIED YOU...
CHRISTMAS CARDS
MERRY
XMAS

IT'S OUR SECOND HONEYMOON, AND WE'RE DOING EVERYTHING EXACTLY AS WE DID ON OUR FIRST—
—MY WIFE IS UPSTAIRS IN BED WITH THE HOTEL MANAGER!

OF COURSE I LOVE YOU-
BUT I CAN'T TAKE
YOU AWAY FROM
YOUR FAMILY...

HAVE A LOVELY HONEYMOON – AND REMEMBER, LOVE MEANS NEVER HAVING TO SAY "YES"!

YOUR "BLIND DATE" SAW YOU THROUGH THE WINDOW – AND SHE'LL SEE YOU AND THE DATING AGENCY IN COURT!

I'VE BEEN WEARING THEM SINCE MY WIFE FOUND THEM IN MY CAR...

I CAN RECOMMEND HAVING A NEW MAN - EVERY NIGHT!

IT'S A GET WELL SOON CARD-
FROM MY HUSBAND'S MISTRESS!

ISN'T HE LOVELY – AND JUST LIKE HIS FATHER – EVEN THE BIRTHMARK ON HIS BOTTOM IS THE SAME...

THESE NEW FASHIONS ARE SO SILLY – CAN YOU SEE ME IN A MINI SKIRT, BLACK STOCKINGS AND A PAIR OF STILETTOS?

I CONVINCED MY HUSBAND I WAS HAVING AN AFFAIR WITH HIS BOSS – WHICH LEAVES ME PLENTY OF TIME TO SECRETLY STUDY FOR MY DEGREE IN NUCLEAR PHYSICS!

– WHY CAN'T YOU JUST BUY ORDINARY CONDOMS LIKE EVERYONE ELSE, AND STOP ALL THIS SHOWING OFF!

MARTIN! I'VE MADE AN APPOINTMENT FOR YOU AT THE SPERM BANK-
THEY ARE GOING TO SHOW YOU HOW TO MAKE A WITHDRAWAL!

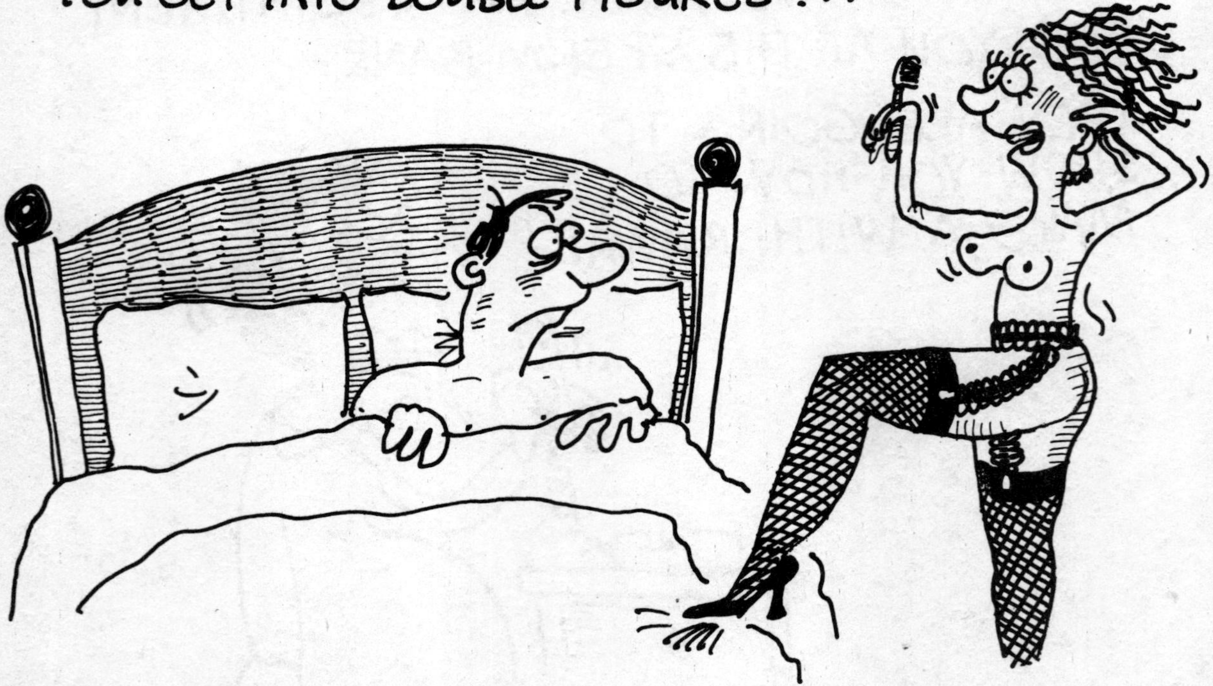

DO YOU WANT A SCORE OUT OF TEN – OR SHALL I MAKE IT A PERCENTAGE TO ENSURE YOU GET INTO DOUBLE FIGURES?..

HONEYMOON HOTEL PLC
-YOU WANT TO SPEAK TO MR. AND MRS. SMITH - CERTAINLY... ... ROOM 5, OR 12, OR 17, OR 26, OR 31, OR 42, OR....
RECEPTION

HONEYMOON IN BARBADOS? SIMPLE! JUST INSIST ON GETTING MARRIED DURING THE CRICKET TOUR SEASON...

IT'S FOR YOU...
FLASH-
-A-GRAM!

WE MAKE LOVE WHENEVER ENGLAND WIN A MATCH – I HAVE SOME LOVELY MEMORIES OF 1966...

OH NO! I DON'T MIND HIM GOING TO THE PUB – I COULDN'T HAVE AN AFFAIR WITH HIM HANGING AROUND HERE EVERY NIGHT!

MR. WILSON – YOUR WIFE JUST CALLED – SHE'S FOUND OUT ABOUT OUR AFFAIR AND WANTS TO KNOW IF YOU WANT YOUR CLOTHES SHREDDED OR BURNED . . .

YES – I LIKE TO WAKE UP FEELING A NEW MAN EVERY MORNING, TOO!

SHE'S NEVER BEEN HAPPY BEING A GOLF WIDOW HAS SHE...

YES, MARTIN, WOMEN DO LIKE MEN WHO CAN MAKE THEM LAUGH...

... BUT THERE'S A TIME AND PLACE FOR IT!..

HE'S THE IMAGE OF HIS FATHER - BUT I COULDN'T LEAVE MY HUSBAND ON OUR HONEYMOON AND RUN OFF WITH A SPANISH WAITER...

I WANT YOU TO MAKE LOVE TO ME LIKE YOU DID IN MY DREAM LAST NIGHT...
...I'LL PUT ON MY STOCKINGS WHILE YOU FETCH MR. WILKINSON FROM NEXT DOOR!

THE SPARKLE HAS GONE OUT OF OUR RELATIONSHIP - HE ONLY EVER WANTS TO MAKE LOVE IN THE BEDROOM THESE DAYS...

THE HONEYMOON'S OVER...

I THINK OUR PROSPECTIVE LADIES WILL WANT A LITTLE MORE THAN SIMPLY "ME, TARZAN..."

IT'S EASY TO TELL YOU WERE AN ONLY CHILD ~
YOU NEVER LEARNED TO COME SECOND...

DIVORCED

YOU BET IT'S GOING TO BE **SAFE SEX** –
YOU BOUGHT **CHEWING GUM**!

SO! WOMEN HAVE NO MECHANICAL APTITUDE?

- AND AFTER THE BREAK WE'LL BE LOOKING AT A SILLY REPORT WHICH CLAIMS THAT SOME T.V. PRESENTERS GET THE JOB THROUGH SEX APPEAL RATHER THAN JOURNALISTIC ABILITY...

–HE'S A MASOCHIST – AND HE'S JUST FOUND OUT THAT HIS WIFE **ISN'T** HAVING AN AFFAIR!

–HE ALWAYS SINGS IN THE BATH – HE THINKS IT COVERS UP THE SOUND OF HIM BREAKING WIND!

DO WE SMOKE AFTER SEX?
NO-I CAN'T RECALL US EVER DOING IT THAT QUICKLY!
SALE
SURVEY

WE'VE BEEN SAVING FOR FIVE YEARS FOR AN EXTENSION - AND THIS IS WHERE WE'RE GOING TO GET IT!

ARE YOU CERTAIN IT'S A HOLD UP? - IT LOOKS LIKE AN ORDINARY STOCKING TO ME!
BUILDING SOCIETY
KAREN

I HATE LEAP YEARS!

IT'S ABOUT TIME YOU MADE SOMETHING OF YOURSELF!

PUT THE MADONNA TAPE ON
AND I'LL SHOW YOU THE DANCE
WE'RE DOING AT THE VILLAGE
FAIR NEXT SATURDAY...

–HOW WAS IT FOR ME? I'LL LET YOU KNOW AFTER I'VE WATCHED THE VIDEO I MADE OF IT!

OH! I **LOVE** HONEYMOONS, DON'T YOU?

NO!!
HOW TO READ MINDS
KAMA SUTRA

YOU'RE NOT TO TAKE THE DOG OUT FOR ANY MORE WALKS...
... THE VET SAYS HE'S ALCOHOLIC...

I SENT MY HUSBAND ON A RELAXATION COURSE... NOW – WHENEVER HE FEELS SEXY – I JUST PUT ON THE RIGHT MOOD MUSIC AND HE FALLS ASLEEP!

I'M VERY INTERESTED IN CURRENT AFFAIRS-
AND I'D LIKE TO GO SOMEWHERE
WHERE I CAN
HAVE ONE!
TRAVEL AGENT
FLY NOW
BUREAU DE CHANGE

COMPUTER DATING!

FRIEND OF THE GROOM?! CERTAINLY NOT!
I'M THE BRIDE'S MOTHER!

WELL – YOU SAID YOU WANTED TO GO SOMEWHERE YOU'VE NEVER BEEN BEFORE...

WELL IT CAN'T BE A HANGOVER – YOU HAVE TO BE SOBER TO HAVE ONE OF THOSE!

OF COURSE YOU'RE NOT OVERWEIGHT DARLING, YOU'RE JUST NOT AS TALL AS YOU SHOULD BE...

SHE'S JUST HAD MAJOR PLASTIC SURGERY –
THE BANK CONFISCATED ALL HER CREDIT CARDS!

I CAN'T STAND THE SIGHT OF YOU ANY LONGER – I AM GOING TO MARRY YOUR TWIN BROTHER.
Sue

HELP ME UPSTAIRS, HENRY, I FEEL LIKE BEING A SEX MACHINE!

IT'S MY TOY BOY ...

OF COURSE I DON'T JUST LOVE YOU BECAUSE YOU WON A MILLION POUNDS ON THE LOTTERY - I'D LOVE YOU JUST AS MUCH IF YOU HAD WON IT ON THE FOOTBALL POOLS...

WELL – IF HE'D BEEN A HORSE I WOULD HAVE HAD HIM PUT DOWN YEARS AGO FOR PERSISTENT REFUSAL !!

HIS WIFE RAN OFF WITH ANOTHER WOMAN-HIS MISTRESS-AND NEITHER OF THEM WILL IRON HIS SHIRTS NOW...

RELAX, MR. WIBLEY, YOU HAVE NO SEXUALLY TRANSMITTED DISEASES - BUT ASK YOUR WIFE TO COME IN FOR AN EXAMINATION ANYWAY AND I WON'T SAY ANYTHING ABOUT THE SHEEP!

BETTER MAKE IT SMOKING - MY WIFE USUALLY HAS A CIGARETTE AFTER SEX...
KWIKFLY AIRLINES
CHECK-IN

WELL - AFTER 26 YEARS OF MARRIAGE AND FOUR CHILDREN WHERE WOULD YOU GO FOR A BIT OF PEACE AND QUIET!

CAN'T TALK NOW – MARTIN WANTS TO MAKE LOVE – CALL YOU BACK IN TWO MINUTES!

– DON'T THEY NORMALLY PUT SECURITY VIDEO CAMERAS ON THE CEILING?!

WELL!
EVERYBODY HAS AT LEAST ONE KINKY HABIT!!

IT WAS LOVE AT SECOND SIGHT – THE FIRST TIME SHE LOOKED SHE DIDN'T KNOW HE WAS A MILLIONAIRE...

MY BOYFRIEND USED TO KISS ME ON THE LIPS-
BUT IT'S ALL OVER NOW!

FORGET IT-SHE USES THE BEST ORAL CONTRACEPTIVE THERE IS-
-SHE ALWAYS SAYS NO!

IF YOU GO BALD AT THE FRONT IT MEANS YOU'RE SEXY -
IF YOU GO BALD AT THE BACK IT MEANS YOU'RE A THINKER -

YOU OBVIOUSLY THINK A LOT ABOUT SEX !

OF COURSE I TALK TO MY HUSBAND WHEN I'M MAKING LOVE – IF HE TELEPHONES...

OF COURSE MY HUSBAND IS A NEW MAN – THE OLD ONE WOULDN'T COOK OR CLEAN.

WELL - I'M SORRY TREVOR, I DON'T REMEMBER ANYTHING IN OUR WEDDING VOWS ABOUT HAVING SEX FOR **FUN**!

MY HUSBAND IS GREAT IN BED – HE SHOULD BE, HE CERTAINLY GETS ENOUGH PRACTISE...

-HIS WIFE'S A SUPERMODEL - ACCIDENTALLY SWALLOWED SOME OF HER LUNCH - SHE'S DOWN IN EMERGENCY LIPOSUCTION...

– THE COMPUTER'S DOWN...

NO - I WOULDN'T WANT A NEW MAN FOR A HUSBAND - I'VE HAD ENOUGH TROUBLE HOUSETRAINING THE OLD ONE!

WERE THERE ANY OTHER MEN IN YOUR LIFE, BEFORE YOU MARRIED ME?

- IGNORE HIM - HE'S JUST PLAYING HARD TO GET!

JUST A MINUTE...
...I AM YOUR HUSBAND!

WOW! THAT'S AMAZING!
- THERE ARE EXACTLY 463 ROSES ON THE WALLPAPER IN THIS BEDROOM!

OH YES!
IT ALWAYS STARTS WHEN YOU SINK INTO HIS ARMS...
...BUT YOU ALWAYS END UP WITH YOUR ARMS IN HIS SINK!

–I THINK WE REALLY NEED TO DEAL WITH YOUR **SHYNESS** PROBLEM, BERYL!

—HELLO, DARLING, YOU'RE HOME EARLY. COME INSIDE AND I'LL TELL YOU ALL ABOUT MY NEW JOB...

PERHAPS YOU SHOULD BE GOING OUT WITH HER THEN!
HAZEL WOOD

MY WIFE WANTS TO MAKE LOVE IN A DIFFERENT PLACE EVERY NIGHT...
... UNFORTUNATELY IT'S NEVER AT HOME...

LEFT A BIT … DOWN A BIT … THAT'S IT …
… THAT'S FOREPLAY!

THEN I SUGGESTED WE MAKE LOVE IN THE BACK OF THE CAR LIKE WE DID BEFORE WE WERE MARRIED...

WE GAVE HIM THE NICKNAME "MR. FLOPPY" FOR AN ENTIRELY DIFFERENT REASON...
COMPUTER SOFTWARE

A FEW CARD TRICKS BEFORE BED WILL NOT PUT THE MAGIC BACK INTO OUR SEX!

NO-NOT A SHOTGUN WEDDING -HER FATHER IS VERY PROGRESSIVE AND MODERN- HE USED AN ELECTRIC CATTLE PROD!

... NO GOOD HIDING – IT'S FRIDAY NIGHT!

OH NO! I DIDN'T DIVORCE HIM BECAUSE HE MADE SEXY VIDEOS OF US ON OUR HONEYMOON...
...IT WAS THE FACT THAT HE WANTED TO GIVE HIS MOTHER AND TWO SISTERS EQUAL STAR BILLING!

LET ME EXPLAIN, MELLORS; IN THIS BED I WEAR THE CAP...

THAT'S A NO THEN?!.

FINDAMATE
...COMPUTER DATING...
-HELLO, MISS. BROWN, JUST RINGING TO CONFIRM THAT THE MEASUREMENT I GAVE YOU SHOULD BE IN INCHES...
... NOT CENTIMETRES!

–AND WATCH OUT FOR MY CAR . . .